1978

Some
Changes

Black Poets Series
Julius Lester,
General Editor

June Jordan
SOME CHANGES

Larry Neal
HOODOO HOLLERIN' BEBOP GHOSTS & OTHER VISIONS

Stanley Crouch
AIN'T NO AMBULANCES FOR NO NIGGUHS TONIGHT

Also by June Jordan
WHO LOOK AT ME

SOULSCRIPT

June Jordan

Some Changes

A Richard W. Baron Book

E. P. Dutton & Co., Inc., New York 1971

Dedicated to new peoplelife
with gratitude to R. Buckminster Fuller

Contents

Three

Four

Introduction

Black poetry. Poetry written by black people as opposed to Negroes and *cullud* people. Poetry written, not with the mind of a white American behind a dark skin, but poetry written by America's internal aliens, the outsiders in America's midst, the black Vietcong. Black poetry. Poetry which speaks to and of the black experience, and the black experience is how blacks experience America and themselves. Thus, the expression of the black experience should illuminate the consciousness of anyone who opens himself to it. Indeed, it affords nonblacks an opportunity to see themselves in a mirror which will not return to them the image they might want to see. And it affords blacks the same experience and more.

June Jordan is a black poet. A black woman poet. That's a devastating combination. To be black and to be a woman. To be a double outsider, to be twice-oppressed, to be more than invisible. June Jordan is a black woman poet. Think about that. A black woman poet. That's triple vision.

As a black woman poet, June Jordan is faithful to the three primary aspects of her being, falsifying nothing. For some, her poetry may not qualify as "black poetry" because she doesn't rage or scream. No, she's quiet, but the intensity is frightening. Her poetry is highly disciplined, highly controlled. It's tight, like the Muddy Waters blues band is tight. There is nothing wasted, and it is impossible to separate what she says from how she says it. Indeed, how she writes is as much what is being said as what is being said intellectually. She isn't concerned with converting the listener (and her poetry must be listened to, not merely read) to a particular point of view. Her concern is the concern of the poet who is also a musician, of the poet for whom words are merely the beginning and not the end of the experience. She wants the listener to feel what she feels, see what she sees, and then do with it what he may. Hopefully, he will become more human, more caring, more intensely alive to the suffering and the joy. Her poems only begin to live in the space around the words, that space representing the spaces inside the listener. A poem only lives when it has a soul to reside in. The poet, however, cannot force these poems into the beings of others. Others have to be willing to take the poems inside. Poetry is not a state, or a thing, or something to be studied. It is a basic form of communication, requiring one who is willing to speak and one who is willing to listen and not fear the consequences of that listening.

What else is there to say? Here're the poems. June Jordan has done what she could. The rest is up to you.

JULIUS LESTER

January, 1970

One

For My Mother

for my mother
I would write a list
of promises so solid
loafing fish and onions
okra palm tree coconut
and Khus-Khus paradise
would
hard among the mongoose
enemies delight
a neo-noon-night trick
prosperity

for my father
I would decorate a doorway
weaving women into the daytime
of his travel also
season the snow to rice and peas
to peppery pearls on a flowering
platter drunkards stilt
at breakfast bacchanalia
swaying swift or stubborn
coral rocks
regenerate

for my only love
I would stop the silence

one of these days

won't come too soon
when the blank
familias blank
will fold away
a highly inflammable
balloon eclipsed by seminal
and nubile

loving

In the Times of My Heart

In the times of my heart
the children tell the clock
a hallelujah
          listen people
          listen

The New Pieta: For the Mothers
and Children of Detroit

They wait like darkness not becoming stars
long and early in a wrong one room
he moves no more

Weeping thins the mouth a poor escape from fire
lights to claim to torch the body
burial by war

She and her knees lock slowly closed (a burning door)
not to continue as they bled before
he moves no more

The Wedding

Tyrone married her this afternoon
not smiling as he took the aisle
and her slightly rough hand.
Dizzella listened to the minister
staring at his wrist and twice
forgetting her name:
Do you promise to obey?
Will you honor humility and love
as poor as you are?
Tyrone stood small but next
to her person
trembling. Tyrone stood
straight and bony
black alone with one key
in his pocket.
By marrying today
they made themselves a man
and woman
answered friends or unknown
curious about the Cadillacs
displayed in front of Beaulah Baptist.
Beaulah Baptist
life in general
indifferent
barely known
nor caring to consider
the earlywed Tyrone
and his Dizzella
brave enough
but only two.

The Reception

Doretha wore the short blue lace last night
and William watched her drinking so she fight
with him in flying collar slim-jim orange
tie and alligator belt below the navel pants uptight

"I flirt. You hear me? Yes I flirt.
Been on my pretty knees all week
to clean the rich white downtown dirt
the greedy garbage money reek.

I flirt. Damned right. You look at me."
But William watched her carefully
his mustache shaky she could see
him jealous, "which is how he always be

at parties." Clementine and Wilhelmina
looked at trouble in the light blue lace
and held to George while Roosevelt Senior
circled by the yella high and bitterly light blue face

he liked because she worked
the crowded room like clay like molding men
from dust to muscle jerked
and arms and shoulders moving when

she moved. The Lord Almighty Seagrams bless
Doretha in her short blue dress
and Roosevelt waiting for his chance:
a true gut-funky blues to make her really dance.

Nowadays the Heroes

Nowadays the heroes go out looking
for the cradle in the cold
explore
a cemetery for beginnings
(irony can kill
                    the children panic at
the research in the glowing graveyard
what
what about
what about humanity in heat
the arms
the sleep alive?)
                    Look.
Look for the life
Look for reflections of the living
real problem:
money is the sun that makes us shine.

Not a Suicide Poem

no one should feel peculiar living
as they do

next door the neighbors rent their windows

formerly a singing
shatters toneless shards
to line an inmost holdup

drivel salt the stinking coin
iconochasmic mire
reedy
dull like alcoholic
holy apostolic hireling
herd
inchoate incompatible
and taxing
toll the holy
tell the hireling

>   alcoholic
>   apostolic
>   tales

terrific reeking epidermal
damage
marrow rot
sebaceous glisten smell
quotidian kaleidoscopic
tricked indecent darling hell

no one should feel peculiar living well

This Man

This old whistle
could not blow
except
to whiskey wheeze
with bandage on his head
temple to temple
black
and dry hands
in his pockets keeping
warm
two trembling fists
clammed
against a stranger
('s) blueandwhite sedan
he
would never drive
could not repair
but damaged
just by standing there.

Fibrous Ruin

Fibrous ruin of the skin not near
not anywhere not torn nor stained
now disappears like leaf and flood

A loose appealing
to the vanishing of many scars lost
by long healing of long loss slipped
quietly across a bruise new broken
from new pain inside
the feeling of let go

Abandoned Baby

Young ash craven
   never near to gold and
   further still from blood

Birth aborted
   risen in that grave of
   other needs dangling

Angles pins and knobs
   discard their use
   to form your tomb

Uncle Bullboy

His brother   after dinner
once a year would play the piano
short and tough in white shirt
plaid suspenders   green tie and
checked trousers.
Two teeth were gold.   His eyes
were pink with alcohol.   His fingers
thumped for Auld Lang Syne.
He played St. Louis Woman
Boogie, Blues, the light
pedestrian.

But one night after dinner
after chitterlings and pigs' feet
after bourbon rum and rye
after turnip greens and mustard greens
and sweet potato pie
Bullboy looking everywhere
realized his brother was not there.

Who would emphasize the luxury
of ice cream by the gallon who would
repeat effusively the glamour not the gall
of five degrees outstanding on the wall?
Which head would nod and then recall
the crimes   the apples stolen from the stalls
the soft coal stolen by the pile?
Who would admire
the eighteenth pair of forty
dollar shoes?
Who could extol their mother with good
brandy as his muse?

His brother   dead from drinking
Bullboy drank to clear his thinking
saw the roach inside the riddle.
Soon the bubbles from his glass
were the only bits of charm
which overcame his folded arms.

Maybe the Birds

Maybe the birds are worried
by the wind

they scream like people
in the hallway

wandering among the walls

In Memoriam: Martin Luther King, Jr.

I

honey people murder mercy U.S.A.
the milkland turn to monsters teach
to kill to violate pull down destroy
the weakly freedom growing fruit
from being born

America

tomorrow yesterday rip rape
exacerbate despoil disfigure
crazy running threat the
deadly thrall
appall belief dispel
the wildlife burn the breast
the onward tongue
the outward hand
deform the normal rainy
riot sunshine shelter wreck
of darkness derogate
delimit blank
explode deprive
assassinate and batten up
like bullets fatten up
the raving greed
reactivate a springtime
terrorizing

by death by men by more
than you or I can

STOP

II

They sleep who know a regulated place
or pulse or tide or changing sky
according to some universal
stage direction obvious

like shorewashed shells

we share an afternoon of mourning
in between no next predictable
except for wild reversal hearse rehearsal
bleach the blacklong lunging
ritual of fright insanity and more
deplorable abortion
more and
more

If You Saw a Negro Lady

If you saw a Negro lady
sitting on a Tuesday
near the whirl-sludge doors of
Horn & Hardart on the main drag
of downtown Brooklyn

solitary and conspicuous as plain
and neat as walls impossible to
fresco and you watched her self-
conscious features shape about
a Horn & Hardart teaspoon
with a pucker from a cartoon

she would not understand
with spine as straight and solid
as her years of bending over floors
allowed

skin cleared of interest by a ruthless
soap   nails square and yellowclean
from metal files

sitting in a forty-year-old flush
of solitude and prickling
from the new white cotton blouse
concealing nothing she had ever noticed
even when she bathed and never
hummed a bathtub tune nor knew one

If you saw her square
above the dirty
mopped-on antiseptic floors
before the rag-wiped table tops

little finger   broad and stiff
in heavy emulation of a cockney

mannerism

would you turn her treat
into surprise by
observing

happy birthday

For Somebody to Start Singing

(Song in Memory of Newark, New Jersey)

He's a man on the roof
on the run with a gun
he's a man

Boys and little girls
they were bad and they were good
now they're dead

He's a man on the roof
on the run with a gun
he's a man

Had no name and looked
the same but today
the soldiers tremble
at his aim

He's a man on the roof
on the run with a gun
he's a man

The country kept baiting
a people kept waiting
they all stood in line
then they left

He's a man on the roof
on the run with a gun
he's a man

If I have to kill myself
gone burn this box burn
all the locks
that keep me out

He's a man on the roof
on the run with a gun
he's a man

And Who Are You?

I

Leave my eyes
alone
why should I make
believe this place entirely

is white
and I am nothing

pasted to a fantasy
(big black phallus
wide white teeth)
of particles you
blast to pieces asking me
to swallow them as
monster bits

That bit is me.

and even if I wave my arms no
rules will stop the traffic
stop the hatred running near
with ropes and mongrels
on the mind blind cloth
and bloodhounds
at the cradle

II

Don't tell me windmills
like the color of maroon
which was OK
when I first saw a zebra

that's the color of her coat
and in the hallway where she
waits for money once a week
she pulls a spool

of silk along the needles

for a doily

don't tell me windmills
turn no more just
like the horse
that used to lead
the trolleys   you can't
help but smell four legs the
board above for two and hear him
bargaining to tune bananamato
peachpotato   awk   awk
parsley

nothing goes too fast

old fish and unwashed hair why
don't he cut the screwing get
him something nice   sits
on the step a
nylon stocking cap to
cover up his head the cat
fastidious outside
the room
of his secondhand bed

        III

Old fish and unwashed hair
you may surmise by reading
the windows
bandaged with the Daily
News from World War
Two which anyway was not the first
that

nothing goes too fast

but slowly like the windmill
like the good milord

and Uncle Remus for a hero

O merrily the children
suffered verily the elevator
Boys with buttons
from the Army and the cleaning
Girls of fifty-five
                    "the children"
suffered as they came to
hear the wild and holy
black book out of the mouths
of the mob and underneath
a hanging tree

          IV

Take the acolyte
obsequious and horsey
under lace
                on Monday
off the altar

on the stoop

and no more candles
in the vestibule a no
watt testicle just dangles

take the acolyte his
yellhello for girls his
little sister slow with shoes from '66
a blue harmonica inside her mouth o
sweetly play that Jesu Joy of
Man's Desiring and Desiring and desiring
she
should comb her hair at least or he
could screw forgiveness
for a change move
over but

don't tell me
drums and muscle

on the stoop

sit-in on the stoop
museum
tombstone of the horse maroon
dark dais insane sanctum
if you make it you play ball
                    talk loud
                    speak low
                    drink cheap
                    tell lies
                    LOOK AT THE PEOPLE

HE LOOKS LIKE A MAN
HE LOOKS LIKE ONE

All the World Moved

All the world moved next to me strange
I grew on my knees
in hats and taffeta trusting
the holy water to run
like grief from a brownstone
cradling.

Blessing a fear of the anywhere
face too pale to be family
my eyes wore ribbons
for Christ on the subway
as weekly as holiness
in Harlem.

God knew no East no West no South
no Skin nothing I learned like
traditions of sin but later
life began and strangely
I survived His innocence
without my own.

Juice of a Lemon on the Trail
of Little Yellow

Little Yellow looked at the banana tree and
he looked at the moon and he heard a banana tree baboon
beneath the moon and he sat on the grass
and fell asleep there

Little Yellow nine years old underneath the moon beside
a big banana tree smiled a mango smile as he
listened to a lullaby palm and a naked woman broke
coconuts for him and fed him meat from her mango
mammaries

Little Yellow curled himself in a large banana leaf
and he deeply sailed asleep toward the mango moon
Little Yellow traveled to a place where coolies worked
to build a bathtub for the rough and tribal Caribbean

There on that lush cerulean plateau and trapped he
was kept by his boss   brother who positively took
out his teeth and left the mango mouth of Little Yellow
empty

I Live in Subtraction

I live in subtraction.
I hide from rain.
I hold the sun with sleep.
I sleep without the stars.
I can even close my eyes.

I live in subtraction.
I forget your name.
I forbid my heart its mind.
I forgive my mind its dream.
I can end a dream with death.

Two

What Declaration

What declaration can I make to clear
this room of strangers leaving
quickly as an enemy might come?
You look at me not knowing
I must guess what question I can ask
to open every mouth (and mine)
to free the throat (and yours) from fear.
We keep unknown to us
and I apart from me will search
my own deliberation my own you
and you and you, my own.

My Sadness Sits Around Me

My sadness sits around me
  not on haunches not in any
  placement near a move
and the tired roll-on
of a boredom without grief

If there were war
I would watch the hunting
I would chase the dogs
and blow the horn
because blood is commonplace

As I walk in peace
  unencountered unmolested
  unimpinging unbelieving unrevealing
  undesired under every 0
My sadness sits around me

Not Looking

Not looking now and then I find you here
not knowing where you are.
Talk to me. Tell me the things I see
fill the table between us or surround
the precipice nobody dares to forget.
Talking takes time takes everything
sooner than I can forget the precipice
and speak to your being there
where I hear you move no nearer
than you were standing on my hands
covered my eyes dreaming about music.

When I or Else

when I or else when you
and I or we
deliberate I lose I
cannot choose if you if
we then near or where
unless I stand as loser
of that losing possibility
that something that I have
or always want more than much
more at
least to have as less and
yes directed by desire

Whereas

Whereas
Judas hung himself
I despise bravura

Whereas
Socrates ignored his wife
I buckle at the brim

Whereas
Judas hung himself
I find no rope as strong

Or

OR
like Atlanta parking lots insatiable
and still
collected kindly by the night

love lies

wrong riding hard
in crazy gear
the hills fly by corruptible
and polar up

and up
the bottom traveling
too proud

Let Me Live with Marriage

Let me live with marriage
as unruly as alive
or else alone and longing
not too long alone.
Love if unduly held by guilt
is guilty with fear
wronging that fixed impulse
to seek and ever more
to bind with love. Oh yes!
I am black within
as is this skin
without one pore
to bleed a pale defense: Will you attack
as cruel
as you claim me cruel? With word with silence
I have flung myself from you. And now
absurd
I sing of stillborn lyrics almost sung.

If this be baffling then the error's proved
To love so long and leave my love unmoved.

Toward a Personal Semantics

if I do take somebody's word on
it means I don't know and you have to
believe if you just don't know

how do I dare to stand as
still as I am still standing

arrows create me
but I am no wish

after all the plunging
myself is no sanctuary
birds feed and fly inside me shattering
the sullen spell of any
accidental

eyeless storm to twist and sting
the tree of my remaining
like the wind

Then It Was

Then it was
our eyes locked slowly
on the pebble wash
of humus leaves and
peeled the plummet belly
of a thundercloud

You bent your neck
beneath a branch my
arms enclosed
and slipped your shadow
over me

Soon we had bathed
the sun fell at our feet
and broke into the sliding
ferment of our warmth

we were an early evening

San Juan

Accidental far into the longer light
or smoking
clouds that lip whole hillsides
spoken nearly foliated full
a free green ravelling alive
as blue as pale
as rectilinear

the red the eyebrow
covering a privacy a space
particular ensnarement
flowering roulette

place opening knees night water

color the engine air
on Sunday
silhouette the sound

and silently

some miles away the mountain
the moon
the same

For Christopher

Tonight
   the machinery of shadow
      moves into the light

He is lying there
      not a true invalid
         not dying

Now his face looks blue
        but all of that small body
        will more than do
           as life.

The lady radiologist
        regardless how and where
           she turns the knob

will never know
        the plenty of pain
             growing

parts to arm
      a man inside the boy

practically asleep

Leaves Blow Backward

leaves blow backward with the wind
behind them beautiful
and almost run through atmosphere
of flying birds
or butterflies turn light
more freely than my mouth
learns to kiss by speaking
among aliens.

Nobody Riding the Roads Today

Nobody riding the roads today
But I hear the living rush
far away from my heart

Nobody meeting on the streets
But I rage from the crowded
overtones of emptiness

Nobody sleeping in my bed
But I breathe like windows
broken by emergencies

Nobody laughing anymore
But I see the world split
and twisted up like open stone

Nobody riding the roads today
But I hear the living rush
far away from my heart

Firing Burst His Head

Firing burst his head
excruciation blasted silly
clay declining
blind development
exploding fragile like the
afternoon

waste   the steeple placement
flesh too hot to last
or thin
no winner knows
the vulnerable victory arriving
dead between the baby hands
unlikely kindred
disappearing

cries around the brighter ravage
relegates an ear alone
an ear afflicted solitary
teach the hollow
formulate crude necrophilia
perhaps

or worse

the phony whining bones
disintegrate to tender tiny now
impossible and true

and true
impossible

In Love

in love

never tired of the forward to retreat
never stayed at the edges
imagining now the full

crack-wrung oblivion rolls
and roars a shifting
certainty

thorns to snare the stars
sea forest firm jaggedly cluster
hard-leaved
bird and bee brambling green
prickle hills of the earth rise
a ready thrust a foamchoke hushing
huge against the tides

galactic gallop leading darkness
to its flourish

indivisible the vision sounding
space enough

enough

affinity and I am
where we want to be

particular and chronic

Three

What Would I Do White?

What would I do white?
What would I do clearly full
of not exactly beans nor
pearls my nose a manicure
my eyes a picture of your wall?

I would disturb the streets by
passing by so pretty kids
on stolen petty cash would look
at me like foreign
writing in the sky

I would forget my furs on any chair.
I would ignore the doormen at the knob
the social sanskrit of my life
unwilling to disclose my cosmetology,
I would forget.

Over my wine I would acquire
I would inspire big returns to equity
the equity of capital I am
accustomed to accept

like wintertime.

I would do nothing.
That would be enough.

Okay "Negroes"

Okay "Negroes"
American Negroes
looking for milk
crying out loud
in the nursery of freedomland:
the rides are rough.
Tell me where you got that image
of a male white mammy.
God is vague and he don't take no sides.
You think clean fingernails crossed legs a smile
shined shoes
a crucifix around your neck
good manners
no more noise
you think who's gonna give you something?

Come a little closer.
Where you from?

For Beautiful Mary Brown:
Chicago Rent Strike Leader

All of them are six
who wait inside that other room
where no man walks but many
talk about the many wars

Your baby holds your laboring arms
that bloat from pulling
up and down the stairs to tell
to call the neighbors: We can fight.

She listens to you and she sees
you crying on your knees or else
the dust drifts from your tongue and almost
she can feel her father standing tall.

Came to Chicago like flies to fish.
Found no heroes on the corner.
Butter the bread and cover the couch.
Save on money.

          Don't
tell me how you wash hope hurt and lose
don't tell me how you
sit still at the windowsill:

you will be god to bless you
Mary Brown.

Solidarity Day, 1968

I

Down
between 2 monuments
the cameras and practically
balloons fried chicken cocktail
shrimp
a crayon poster megaphones
police

along the side as always
if you knew them
people

live like pigs

the children bruised and bare and brown
and big enough to know about a bitterness
from rats preoccupied by
helpless competition

the fetter crazy male and female
blue green purple black revolving
slowly holy/brief
battalions limited to tear the entrails
clean like food
somebody grew

for garbage

II

american proximity a zebra

zoo the miserable journeymen
the jackass caravan

yeah yeah

show the sharks their carnage
look at that
humility in hunger

marks the moment of the mud

III

in the kitchen listening
a child sits at a table
steps away from basement stairs
his parents carry ashes
up
his parents rising from the cellar
hold on lug the heavy
heaving holdon lift
the buckets

carry through the ashes

IV

Resurrection died
but not like Jesus only
nailed and crucified

resurrection died
all during the rain
and right among the roses
and under wonderful trees

resurrection died
in full consideration of various
proposals here set forth
or there further considered
or in dedicated statements of nevertheless
never and no
in overweight in ties
in musical clock alarms
in uniform in limousines
in wellattended classrooms
and in ordinary church
from coast to coast

on holiday
on little more than grits
and other bits of boomerang bravado

resurrection went the way the money's spent
on d, e, dash, dash, ashes.

LBJ: Rejoinder

The President talks about peril
to Negroes talking about power
and all I want to say
to him The President
(no less)
until we sway as many
people as he can scare
until we tell
and compel as loud and
as much as The Lonestar
State is large:
"Don't warn me Big
Buddy you have kept me
in my peril long enough you
been pushing Hush My Mouth on me
my lips been black and very blue
but nothing
else than now but power now
and nothing else
will warn
or worry you."

He lost the peace so
he can keep the peril he
knows war is nothing like please.

Poem for My Family: Hazel Griffin and Victor Hernandez Cruz

Dedicated to Robert Penn Warren

I

December 15, 1811
a black, well-butchered slave
named George took leave of Old Kentucky—true
he left that living hell in pieces—
first his feet fell to the fire
and the jelly of his eyes lay smoking
on the pyre a long while—
but he burned complete
at last he left at least he got away.
The others had to stay there
where he died like meat
(that slave)

how did he live?

December 15, 1811

Lilburn Lewis and his brother
cut and killed somebody real
because they missed their mother:
Thomas Jefferson's sweet sister Lucy
Correction: Killed no body: killed a slave
the time was close to Christmas sent the poor
black bastard to the snow zones of a blue-eyed
heaven and he went the way he came like meat
not good enough to eat
not nice enough to see
not light enough to live
he came the way he went like meat.
POEM FOR 175 Pounds
("Poor George")

II

Southern Kentucky, Memphis, New Orleans,
Little Rock, Milwaukee, Brooklyn, San Antonio,
Chicago, Augusta.
I am screaming
do you hear the pulse
destroying properties
of your defense against me and my life

54

now what are you counting
                        dollar bills or lives?
How did you put me down
as property?
as life?
How did you describe the damage?
I am naked
I am Harlem and Detroit
currently knives and bullets
I am lives
YOUR PROPERTY IS DYING
I am lives
MY LIFE IS BEING BORN
This is a lesson
in American History
What can you teach me?
The fire smells of slavery.

III

Here is my voice the speed and the wondering
darkness of my desire is
all that I am here
all that you never allowed:
I came and went like meat not good enough to eat
remember no remember
yes remember me
the shadow following your dreams
the human sound that never reached your ears
that disappear
vestigial
when the question is my scream
and I am screaming
whiteman
do you hear the loud
the blood, the real hysteria of birth
my life is being born
your property is dying

IV

What can you seize
from the furnace
what can you save?
America
I mean America how
do you intend to incinerate
my slavery?
I have taken my eyes from the light of your fires.
The begging body grows cold.
I see.
I see my self
Alive
A life

Uhuru in the O.R.

The only successful heart transplant, of the first five attempts,
meant that a black heart kept alive a white man—a white
man who upheld apartheid.

I like love anonymous
more than murder incorporated or
shall we say South Africa
I like the Valentine the heart the power
incorruptible but failing body
flowers of the world

From my death the white man
takes new breath he stands as
formerly he stood and he commands me
for his good he overlooks
my land my people
in transition transplantations
hearts   and power
beating beating beating beating
hearts in transplantation
power in transition

Four

New Like Nagasaki Nice Like Nicene

Out of the marketplace where
would I go?
Even Holy Communion and I met
my Host across the counter
there in Brooklyn High
Episcopalian
incense of expensive rites
I bowed my braided hair
and held my head as low
as all the rules

I believe the bedside
manner of the church
within the temples full of
gold I believe the gold the
body and the blood let in my name
as citizen belonging to the marketplace
I believe the sale and take the credit
as it comes

Jesus Christ
or God
the creed expands as progress moves
along in step like soldiers
marching everywhere at once
the unsung partners of the great
big bigger biggest button
manufacturers
more buttons for the uniform
shroud paring of the profits from
the boys who wear the flags and
off-days flip their zippers to half-
mast the boys who
fly the planes that kill
the children
over there.

I believe the boys the planes the
button for the uniform the gory raiment
I believe that anyone can be a Christian
like a camera let's

reverse morality read right
to left what else
beside the marketplace what else?
Where would I go? And think about it:

Why would I know your name?

Bus Window

bus window
show himself a
wholesale florist rose somebody
help the wholesale
dollar blossom spill to soil
low pile
on wanton windowsills
whole
saleflorists seedy
decorations startle   small

No Train of Thought, April 4, 1969

A year runs long enough
from force momentum trips
the memory

hard dark tracks

rush hatred hearts
nobody destination
home away

parallels to scare the starting place
start
tracks together
hard dark real long bloody tracks

pull pointless

killers
kill people pointless
killing (people) life
killing (people) love
killing (people)

partly (   )

killing

all of us (   )

Poem from the Empire State

Three of us went to the top of the city
a friend, my son, and I
on that day when winter wrote like snow
across the moonlike sky
and stood there breathing a heavy height
as wide as the streets to see
so poor and frozen far below
that nothing would change for you and me
that swallowing death lay wallowing still
with the wind at the bloat of piled-up swill.
And that was the day we conquered the air
with 100,000 tons of garbage.

No rhyme can be said
where reason has fled.

47,000 Windows

*The Lower East Side of New York City offers, in itself, a
history of American contradiction, devotion to profit, and the
failure of environmental design for human life. People had to
pass a law in order that ventilation and minimal, natural light
be available to the immigrants who had no money for decent
housing. Instead of tearing down the tenements that were
unfit for human habitation, when they were first erected, the
reformers satisfied themselves by legislating phony windows
blasted into the bricks. That was a hundred years ago. Peo-
ple still have to live in those Lower East Side hellholes. This
is a poem about the law that passed some light and air into
that deliberated slum.*

1. There were probably more Indians alive
    than Jews and Italians in that whole
    early American place of New York
    when the city began being big:
    a perfect convergency confirmed
    congested with trade
    creating tolerance for trade requires
    abject curiosity or general indifference
    to anything that sells not well enough
    to tell somebody else about it. And
    at the beginning of New York
    the world was selling well and so was
    tolerance along with trade that
    provocation to a polyethnic population
    trading every bit of time for money
    made the city made me take
    your eye for mine according to extreme
    prosperity and appetite

2. In 1830 then the blurring crowd
    that overwhelming beggarly blur of people came
    they pushed into the seaport cornucopia of New York
    small many people forced
    from land from farms from food from family forced
    small many people left their universe inherited
    like seasons dictatorial

the people fled
political hostilities and hunger
people fled
that soon consuming triumph
of elimination
that machinery for triumph
by a few

3. Then in 1830 the Astors and the Vanderbilts left.
    They rode by carriage from the uproar
    trouble from arrival by the millions
    shoved their ships that wandered
    with the sea to make their glad delivery
    of travelers penniless and hellbent toward
    the welcoming coast of always America

    Those other ones
    they came
    not trading things
    but lives.

4. Unskilled millions crammed old mansions
    broke apart large rooms and took a corner
    held a place a spot a bed a chair a box
    a looking glass
    and kept that space (except for death)
    a safety now for fugitives
    from infamy and famine
    working hard to live.

5. In place of land that street the outhouse
    tenement testimonies
    to a horrifying speculation that would quarter
    and condemn
    debase and shadow and efface
    the privacies of human being

6. Real estate arose as profit spread
    to mutilate the multitudes and kill them
    living just to live.

What can a man survive?
They say: The poor persist.

7. O the Chinese and the Irish and the names!
    The names survived.
    Likewise some families.

8. 1867 after the first and only Civil War
    men looked at others
    men again
    not targets.
    Looked at latrines six stories high
    people paralyzed by penury immobilized
    and children docked
    and hopes untied and
    lying loose and less than skeleton
    at the dirty waters
    by the building of a dollarbill
    venality
    near to nothing
    at the doorway nothing
    only life and speculation:
    What can a man survive?

9. Men looked at other men again
    not targets
    and in 1869 they passed a law
    about the nightmare rising as they saw
    sick men and women nurse their babies
    although love
    is not enough to eat.

10. The Tenement Act of 1869
    was merciful, well-meant, and fine
    in its enforcement
    tore 47,000 windows out of hellhole
    shelter of no light.

    It must be hard to make a window.

What Happens

What happens when the dog sits on a tiger
when the fat man sells a picture of himself
when a lady shoves a sword inside her
when an elephant takes tea cups from the shelf

or the giant starts to cry
and the grizzly loses his grip
or the acrobat begins to fly
and gorillas run away with the whip

What happens when a boy sits on a chair
and watches all the action on the ground and
        in the air
or when the children leave the greatest
        show on earth
and see the circus?

Clock on Hancock Street

In the wintertime my father wears a hat
a green straw laundry shrunken hat
to open up the wartime iron gate
requiring a special key he keeps
in case he hears the seldom basement bell
a long key cost him seven dollars
took three days to make

around the corner

in the house no furniture remains
he gave away the piano
and the hard-back parlor couch the rosy rug
and the double bed
the large black bureau
china cups and saucers
from Japan

His suitcase is a wooden floor
where magazines called *Life*
smell like a garbage truck
that travels farther than he
reasonably can expect
to go

His face seems small or
loose and bearded in the afternoon

Today he was complaining about criminals:

They will come and steal the heavy red umbrella stand

from upstairs in the hallway
where my mother used to walk

and talk to him

Exercise in Quits
(November 15, 1969)

I

                    moratorium means well what
you think it means you
dense? Stop it means stop.

We move and we march sing songs
move march sing songs move march move

It/stop means stop.

                    hey mister man

how long you been fixing to kill somebody?
Waste of time
                    the preparation training

you was born a bullet.

II

we be wondering what they gone do
all them others left and right
what they have in mind

about us
and who by the way is "us"

listen you got a match you got the light
you got two eyes two hands
why you taking pictures of the people
what you sposed to be you
got to photograph the people?

you afraid you will (otherwise) forget
what people look like?

man
or however you been paying dues

we look like you

                on second thought
there is a clear resemblance to the dead
among the living so

go ahead go on   .
and take my picture

quick

A Poem for All the Children

The kind of place for sale big cities
where no gateways wide to greet
or terminate the staying there
persist

you keep it
we can corner what we need

The kind of place for sale the price tag
trees the price tag waters of the land the price
tag lighting of a life the cold cash
freeze on filth

                              o freedom days

The mind or face for sale insensate
supermarket ghostly frozen canned
wrapped-up well-labeled on the counter
always counter-top

The mind or face for sale delivers
hardhead hothouse whoring
homicidal mainly boring
laughter skull

take them things away
we got that   we got that

That place that mind that face
that hereditary rich disgrace

disturbs the triumph
turns the trust disgusting

books that lie and lullabye
schools of enemies and fools

the grownup grab thrownup
blownup

long live the child
love bless the wild

lord lord the older deadly life
the deadly older
lord lord

stale dues. no news. no sale

Cameo No. I

Abraham Lincoln shit he never walked nowhere to read
a book tell all about it all about
the violation the continuous the fuck my face
the dark and evil dark is evil no good dark
the evil and continuous
the light the white the literature he read was
lying blood to leech the life away

believe the Abraham the Lincoln log the literature
the books he read the book he wrote down put
down
put you on the rawhide prairie
emancipated proclamating
Illinois the noise
the boombang bothering my life
the crapcrashchaos print the words
the sprightly syllable destruction
nobody black black nobody black nobody
black
nobody

man

he no Abraham no kind
a president a power walk the miles and read the piles of
pages pale to murder real

                      no wonder he was so depressed

that character
cost me almost
my whole
future   times

Cameo No. II

The name of this poem is

George Washington
somebody want me to think he bad

he bad

George Washington the father of this country
the most the first the holy-poly ghost
the father of this country
took my mother

anyway you want to take that

George the father hypocrite
his life some other bit
than freedom down to every man

George Washington he think he big
he trade my father for a pig

his ordinary
extraordinary human
slaves 300 people Black
and bleeding life beholden to the Presidential
owner underneath the powder of his wicked wig
he think he big

he pulled a blackman from his pocket
put a pig inside the other one
George Washington

the father of this country
stocked
by declarations at the auction block

Prez Washington he say
"give me niggers
let me pay

by check"
(Check the father of this country
what he say:)

"I always pay for niggers
let them stay
like vermin
at Mount Vernon"

impeccable in battle
ManKill Number One
the revolutionary head
aristocratic raider at the vulnerable
slavegirl bed

Americanus Rex
Secretus Blanco-Bronco-Night-Time-Sex

the father of this country
leading privileges of rape and run

George Washington

somebody tell me how he bad he big

I know how he
the great great great great
great great proto-

typical

I Celebrate the Sons of Malcolm

I celebrate the sons of Malcolm
multiplying powerful
implicit
passionate and somber
                    Celebrate
the sons of Malcolm gather
black unruly as alive and hard
against the papal skirts the palace
walls collapsing
                    Celebrate
the sons of Malcolm hold my soul
alert to children building
temples on their feet to face the
suddenly phantom terrors
                    Celebrate
the sons of Malcolm fathering the person
destinies arouse a royal yearning
culminate magnificent
and new

In My Own Quietly Explosive Here

In my own quietly explosive here
all silence isolates
to kill the artificial suffocates
a hunger

Likely dying underground
in circles hold together
wings
develop still regardless

Of Faith: Confessional

silence polishing the streets to rain
who walk the waters
side by side

or used to dance apart
a squaretoe solo stunt
apart
ran stubbornly to pantomime
a corpse

show shadows of the deafman
yesterday the breathing broke
to blow some light against the walls

tomorrow drums the body into birth
a symbol of the sun
entirely alive

a birth to darkness

furnace rioting inside the fruit-rim ribs
dogeaten at the garden gate
but better than the other
early bones
that made the dog eat dog
that made the man smash man

catastrophe

far better
better bones

establishing

a second starting
history

a happiness

Poem to the
Mass Communications Media

I long to fly vast feathers past your mouths on mine
I will to leave the language of the bladder

live yellow and all waste

I will to be

I have begun

I am speaking for

my self

Last Poem for a Little While

I

Thanksgiving 1969
Dear God I thank you for the problems that are mine
and evidently mine alone

By mine I mean just ours
crooked perishable blue like blood
problems yielding to no powers
we can muster we can only starve or stud
the sky the soil the stomach of the human hewn

II

(I am in this crazy room
where people all over the place
look at people all over the place.
For instance Emperors in Bronze Black Face
Or Buddha Bodhisattva sandstone trickled old and dirty into
        inexpensive, public space.)

Insanity goes back a long time I suppose.
An alien religion strikes me lightly
And I wonder if it shows
then how?

III

Immediately prior to the messed-up statues that inspire
monographs and fake mistakes
the Greco-Roman paraplegic tricks
the permanently unbent knee
that indoor amphitheater that celebrates the amputee—

Immediately prior to the messed-up statues
just before the lucratively mutilated choir
of worthless lying recollection

There the aged sit and sleep;
for them museum histories spread too far too deep
for actual exploration

(aged men and women) sit and sleep
before the costly exhibition can begin

to tire what remains of life.

IV

If love and sex were easier
we would choose something else
to suffer.

V

Holidays do loosen up the holocaust
the memories (sting tides) of rain and refuge
patterns hurt across the stranger city
holidays do loosen up the holocaust
They liberate the stolen totem tongue

The cripples fill the temple
palace entertainment under glass
the cripples crutching near the columns swayed
by plastic wrap
disfiguring haven halls or veils the void
impromptu void
where formerly
Egyptian sarcasucker or more recently
where European painting
turns out nothing
no one
I have ever known.

These environments these
artifacts facsimiles these
metaphors these
earrings vase that sword
none of it
none of it
is somehow what I own.

VI

Symbols like the bridge.
Like bridges generally.
Today a flag a red and white and blue new flag
confused the symbols in confusion
bridge over the river
flag over the bridge
The flag hung like a loincloth flicked in drag.

VII

Can't cross that bridge. You listen
things is pretty bad
you want to reach New Jersey
got to underslide the lying spangled banner.
Bad enough New Jersey.
Now Songmy.
Songmy. A sorrow song. Songmy.
The massacre of sorrow songs.
Songmy. Songmy. Vietnam.
Goddamn. Vietnam.
I would go pray about the bridge.
I would go pray a sorrow Songmy song.
But last time I looked the American flag was flying
from the center of the crucifix.

VIII

"Well, where you want to go?"
he asks. "I don't know. It's a long
walk to the subway."
"Well," he says, "there's nothing at home."
"That's a sure thing," she answers.
"That's a sure thing: Nothing's at home."

IX

Please pass the dark meat.
Turkey's one thing I can eat
and eat.
eeney eeney meeney mo
It's hard to know

84

whether I should head into
a movie
or take the highway to the airport.
Pass the salt.
Pass the white meat.
Pass the massacre.
o eeney eeney myney mo.
How bad was it, exactly?
What's your evidence?
Songmy o my sorrow
eeney meeney myney mo
Please pass the ham.
I want to show
Vietnam how we give thanks
around here.
Pass the ham.
And wipe your fingers on the flag.

X

Hang my haven
Jesus Christ
is temporarily off
the wall.

XI

American existence twists
you finally
into a separatist.

XII

I am spiders
on the ceiling of a shadow.

XIII

Daumier was not mistaken.
Old people sleep with their mouths open
and their hands closed flat
like an empty wallet.

So do I.

JUNE JORDAN is a New Yorker, born in Harlem and raised in Bedford-Stuyvesant. She studied at Barnard College and the University of Chicago. She has worked as research associate and writer for the Technical Housing Department of Mobilization for Youth, she has taught English at the City College of New York, Connecticut College, and Sarah Lawrence College, and she is co-director of a creative-writing workshop for children in Brooklyn. She has read her poetry at schools and colleges around the country, and the Academy of American Poets has sponsored her poetry readings throughout New York City public schools and at the Guggenheim Museum. Her poems have been published in *Negro Digest* and *Liberator* and in two anthologies, *The New Black Poetry* and *In the Time of Revolution*. Her articles and essays have appeared in *The New York Times, Partisan Review, Mademoiselle, Esquire, The Nation, Evergreen Review,* and *The Village Voice.* SOME CHANGES is her second book. It was preceded in 1969 by *Who Look At Me,* a poem accompanied by paintings, dedicated to the life of black Americans. She has edited an anthology called *soulscript,* and is at work on a novel. For 1960-70 she held a Rockefeller Foundation fellowship in creative writing and for 1970-71 was awarded the Prix de Rome in Environmental Design of the American Academy in Rome. Despite the title of the last poem in SOME CHANGES, June Jordan also continues to write poetry.

by **JUNE JORDAN**, author of the acclaimed *Who Look at Me*, is the first volume in the important new Black Poets series edited by Julius Lester.

"As a black woman poet, June Jordan is faithful to the three primary aspects of her being, falsifying nothing. For some, her poetry may not qualify as 'black poetry' because she doesn't rage or scream. No, she's quiet, but the intensity is frightening. Her poetry is highly disciplined, highly controlled. It's tight, like the Muddy Waters Blues Band is tight. There is nothing wasted, and it is impossible to separate what she says from how she says it. Indeed, how she writes is as much what is being said as what is being said intellectually. She isn't concerned with converting the listener (and her poetry must be listened to, not merely read) to a particular point of view. Her concern is the concern of the poet who is also a musician, of the poet for whom words are merely the beginning and not the end of the experience. She wants the listeners to feel what she feels, see what she sees, and then do with it what he may. Hopefully, he will become more human, more caring, more intensely alive to the suffering and the joy."

—from the Introduction by
Julius Lester